The WORLD of INSECTS

HELPFUL AND HARMFUL INSECTS

Molly Aloian & Bobbie Kalman

Crabtree Publishing Company

www.crabtreebooks.com

HELPFUL AND HARMFUL
INSECTS

Created by Bobbie Kalman

Dedicated by Vanessa Parson-Robbs
For my parents Ken and Cindy, whose love, strength, and kindness inspire me

Editor-in-Chief
Bobbie Kalman

Writing team
Molly Aloian
Bobbie Kalman

Substantive editor
Kathryn Smithyman

Editors
Kristina Lundblad
Kelley MacAulay
Reagan Miller
Rebecca Sjonger

Design
Margaret Amy Reiach
Samantha Crabtree (cover)
Mike Golka (series logo)

Production coordinator
Katherine Kantor

Photo research
Crystal Foxton

Consultant
Patricia Loesche, Ph.D., Animal Behavior Program,
Department of Psychology, University of Washington

Special thanks to
Virginia Mainprize, Aimee Lefebvre, Alissa Lefebvre,
and Centers for Disease Control and Prevention (CDC)

Illustrations
Barbara Bedell: pages 10, 27 (mosquito), 31 (flower)
Katherine Kantor: page 5 (dragonfly)
Vanessa Parson-Robbs: pages 7, 17 (candle), 20, 21, 27 (louse), 31 (candle)
Margaret Amy Reiach: pages 5 (ant), 11, 25 (magnifying glass)
Bonna Rouse: pages 5 (honeybee), 9, 13, 14, 17 (honeybees), 23, 25 (flea),
   27 (flea), 31 (all except candle and flower)

Photographs
Bruce Coleman Inc.: Robert Gossington: page 28
© CDC: James Gathany: page 26
Omni Photo Communications Inc./Index Stock: page 15
Bobbie Kalman: page 21
James Kamstra: page 19 (top)
Robert McCaw: pages 10, 11, 12 (bottom), 20
Minden Pictures: Mitsuhiko Imamori: page 29 (bottom)
© stephenmcdaniel.com: pages 17, 23
Other images by Brand X Pictures, Corel, Digital Stock, Digital Vision,
   Otto Rogge Photography, and Photodisc

Crabtree Publishing Company
www.crabtreebooks.com   1-800-387-7650

Copyright © **2005 CRABTREE PUBLISHING COMPANY**.
All rights reserved. No part of this publication may be
reproduced, stored in a retrieval system or be transmitted in
any form or by any means, electronic, mechanical, photocopying,
recording, or otherwise, without the prior written permission
of Crabtree Publishing Company. In Canada: We acknowledge the
financial support of the Government of Canada through the Book
Publishing Industry Development Program (BPIDP) for our
publishing activities.

Cataloging-in-Publication Data
Aloian, Molly.
  Helpful and harmful insects / Molly Aloian & Bobbie Kalman.
    p. cm. -- (The world of insects series)
  Includes index.
  ISBN-13: 978-0-7787-2341-7 (RLB)
  ISBN-10: 0-7787-2341-0 (RLB)
  ISBN-13: 978-0-7787-2375-2 (pbk.)
  ISBN-10: 0-7787-2375-5 (pbk.)
  1. Insect pests--Juvenile literature. 2. Beneficial insects--Juvenile literature.
I. Kalman, Bobbie. II. Title.
  SB931.3.A46 2005
  632'.7--dc22
                                                    2005000494
                                                    LC

**Published in
the United States**
PMB16A
350 Fifth Ave.
Suite 3308
New York, NY
10118

**Published
in Canada**
616 Welland Ave.,
St. Catharines, Ontario
Canada
L2M 5V6

**Published in the
United Kingdom**
73 Lime Walk
Headington
Oxford
OX3 7AD
United Kingdom

**Published
in Australia**
386 Mt. Alexander Rd.,
Ascot Vale (Melbourne)
VIC 3032

Contents

What are insects?

Insects are animals. They are **invertebrates**. Invertebrates are animals that have no **backbones**. A backbone is a group of bones in the middle of an animal's back.

Insects are arthropods

Insects belong to a big group of invertebrates called **arthropods**. All arthropods have hard coverings called **exoskeletons**. An exoskeleton covers an insect's whole body. It even covers its legs and head! The exoskeleton protects the insect's body like a suit of armor.

*An insect's exoskeleton is made of a hard material called **chitin**.*

An insect's body

An insect's body has three main sections. The three sections are the head, the **thorax**, and the **abdomen**. All insects have six legs. The legs are attached to the thorax.

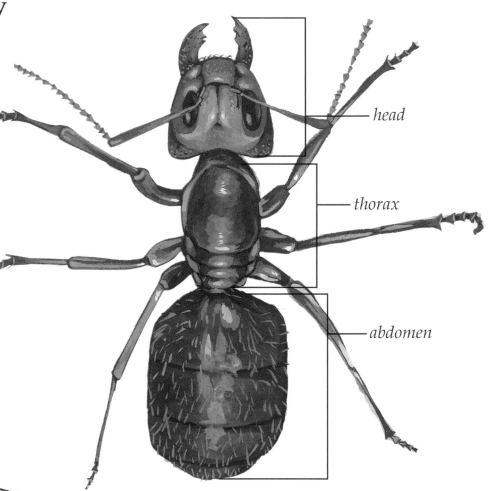

head

thorax

abdomen

A dragonfly has two pairs of wings.

A honeybee has one pair of wings.

Did you know?

Most insects have wings. Some insects have one pair of wings. Others have two pairs of wings. Wings are attached to an insect's thorax. Insects use their wings to fly from place to place.

Helpful or harmful?

Many insects are helpful to other living things. For example, insects are food for many animals. Without insects, the animals would not have enough food to eat! Insects also help plants. Some plants need **pollen** from other plants to make seeds. Without seeds, new plants could not grow. Insects such as bees and butterflies carry pollen from one plant to another.

Insect pests

Not all insects are helpful to other living things. Many people believe that certain insects are harmful. They call these insects **pests**. Some pests eat **crops**. Crops are plants that people grow for food. Other pests bite or sting people.

*Cockroaches can be pests when they live in people's homes. These insects can carry **germs** that make people sick.*

A wasp is an insect that can sting. Most people stay away from wasps because they do not want to be stung.

Eating and being eaten

Insect herbivores eat a lot of plants! Most insect herbivores eat only certain parts of plants. Some eat only leaves. Others eat stems or flowers.

All animals must eat to survive. Animals that eat plants are called **herbivores**. Animals that eat other animals are called **carnivores**. Some animals eat both plants and animals. They are called **omnivores**.

What do insects eat?
Grasshoppers, crickets, and katydids are herbivores. They feed on leaves and stems. Praying mantises, such as the one shown left, and certain flies are carnivores. They feed on other animals, including other insects! Ants are omnivores. They eat both plants and other animals.

Food for many animals

Dragonflies and wasps are insects that eat other insects. Spiders, scorpions, shrews, bats, birds, frogs, and lizards are other animals that eat insects. Without insects, these animals would not have enough food to eat.

Many spiders eat insects. This spider has captured a moth in its web.

Did you know?

Certain kinds of plants are carnivores. Pitcher plants and Venus flytraps are carnivores that eat insects. These plants trap and eat flies, wasps, and ants.

A pitcher plant, shown right, has a pool of liquid at the bottom of its leaves. Insects fall into the liquid and drown.

These aphids are sucking the juices from a milkweed. When the milkweed juices are gone, the plant dies.

Pest Control

Some insects help people and other living things by eating pests. Without these helpful insects, there would be too many pests!

Ladybugs to the rescue!
Ladybugs are helpful insects because they eat aphids. Aphids are tiny insects that suck the juices of plants. Some people believe aphids are pests because aphids eat the plants that people grow. Aphids also feed on milkweeds, which are important foods for other insects. By eating aphids, ladybugs prevent plants from being damaged.

Food for caterpillars

Monarch butterflies lay their eggs only on milkweed leaves. Caterpillars hatch from the eggs that were laid by the monarch butterflies. Monarch caterpillars eat only milkweed.

Helping monarchs

Ladybugs help monarch butterflies and caterpillars by eating aphids. Without ladybugs, there might not be enough places for monarch butterflies to lay eggs. Monarch caterpillars would not have enough milkweed to eat.

Monarch caterpillars need to eat milkweed so they can become monarch butterflies!

11

Cleaning Up

This burying beetle is a scavenger.
It is eating the body of a dead animal.

Scavengers are animals that eat dead or dying plants and animals. Some also eat animal wastes. Scavengers help keep natural areas clean. Without scavengers, waste would pile up on the ground. New plants might not have enough room to grow. Waste from dead things can also make other living things sick.

These green bottle flies are scavengers. They are feeding on a dead fish.

Did you know?

Dung beetles are scavengers. They feed on animal droppings. Female dung beetles lay their eggs inside the droppings. Baby dung beetles, called **larvae**, hatch from the eggs. As soon as the larvae hatch, they start feeding on the droppings. Dung beetles are helpful insects because they eat something that very few other animals eat.

Dung beetles use their legs to roll animal droppings into tight balls. Female dung beetles then lay their eggs inside the balls. The larvae that hatch from the eggs do not have to go far to eat their first meals!

Pollinating plants

Insects help spread pollen from plant to plant. Moving pollen from one plant to another is called **pollination**. When bees and other insects land on flowers to drink **nectar** or eat pollen, some of the pollen in the flowers rubs off on their bodies. The bee shown above is covered in pollen. The bee will carry the pollen to the next flower on which it lands, and pollination will take place.

Looks and smells

Plants that need insects to pollinate them usually have brightly colored flowers and sweet **scents**, or smells. Having bright colors and sweet scents lets insects know that flowers have pollen or nectar. As insects fly from flower to flower to eat, they pollinate the flowers.

Did you know?

Many of the fruits and vegetables that people eat need insects to pollinate the plants on which the fruits and vegetables grow. Oranges, onions, and strawberries grow on plants that insects pollinate. Without insects, the plants might not grow.

*This butterfly is feeding on the nectar of an apple **blossom**, or flower. As the butterfly eats, it pollinates the flower. The apple tree could not grow apples without pollination.*

Busy bees!

*A honeybee has a long, thin tube called a **proboscis** on its head. It uses its proboscis to suck up nectar from flowers.*

Certain insects are helpful in many ways. Honeybees pollinate flowers, but they also make honey and **beeswax** inside their bodies. People eat honey, and they use beeswax to make candles, crayons, and even some candies!

Keeping the bees

Most honeybees make nests called **hives**. Other honeybees live in hives that **beekeepers** build for them. These hives are called **apiaries**. The honeybees leave the apiaries to collect nectar from flowers. They bring the nectar back and turn it into honey. The honey feeds all the bees in the apiaries.

Storing up

The honeybees store their honey in small **cells** inside the apiaries. There are hundreds of cells in each apiary. When the cells are full of honey, the bees cover them with caps made of beeswax.

Gathering honey and wax

When it is time to gather the honey, beekeepers slice off the wax caps. They then remove the honey from the cells. The beekeepers keep the wax, as well. Some beekeepers sell the honey and beeswax at markets. Others sell the honey and beeswax to factories.

Honeybees make a lot more honey than they need! This beekeeper is collecting the beeswax and honey that the honeybees are not using.

Dirt movers

Millions of termites are living inside this termite nest.

Some kinds of ants and termites are helpful because they dig through soil as they build their nests. Digging through soil helps keep the soil **fertile**. Fertile soil is full of **nutrients**. Nutrients are natural substances that help plants and animals grow and stay healthy. Many plants can grow in fertile soil. These plants feed all kinds of animals, including several types of insects!

Mixing it up

Deep layers of soil often have a lot of nutrients. As ants and termites dig, they push up the deep layers of soil to the top of the ground. They mix the layers of soil together. Mixing the soil helps keep the top layers fertile.

Ants use their legs to dig into the soil.

Silk makers

Silkworm caterpillars are helpful to people. Just before they turn into adult butterflies or moths, the caterpillars spin **cocoons** made of **silk** around themselves. All caterpillars make silk inside their bodies, but silkworm caterpillars spin soft silk cocoons. People use this silk to make material for clothing. The material they make is also called silk.

This giant silkworm caterpillar is spinning a silk cocoon around itself.

Silky soft spinners

Certain kinds of silkworm caterpillars are **domestic animals**. Domestic animals are raised and cared for by people. Mulberry silkworm caterpillars are domestic. Most silk clothing is made in factories from the cocoons of mulberry silkworm caterpillars. Silk clothing is shiny, strong, and soft.

These girls are wearing silk blouses.

Did you know?

A silkworm caterpillar can spin about six inches (15.2 cm) of silk in one minute! One long thread of silk comes out of the caterpillar's mouth. People use the silk to make dresses, pajamas, scarves, bed sheets, ties, and curtains. Over 1,000 silk cocoons are needed to make enough fabric for just one silk dress!

21

It stings!

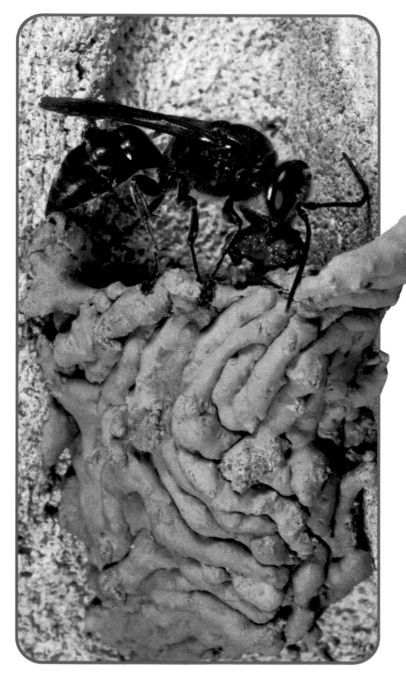

This wasp is making a nest. Wasps often sting people or other animals that disturb their nests.

Many of the things that insects do are helpful to people. Insects sometimes do things that are harmful to people, however. Insects can be harmful when they sting. Insects sting only to protect themselves or to kill other animals for food.

Ouch and itch

Insects that sting poke their **stingers** into other animals. They pump in **venom**, or poison. The venom causes a stinging feeling. Insect stings often become red. They also hurt, itch, and swell.

Did you know?

Some stinging insects are able to sting just one time. Female honeybees can sting only once, and then they die. Other stinging insects can sting more than once. Yellow jackets, hornets, and wasps can sting over and over again.

stinger

After a female honeybee stings, she flies away. As she flies away, her stinger tears away from her body. The honeybee dies soon after she has stung an animal or person.

Bad bites

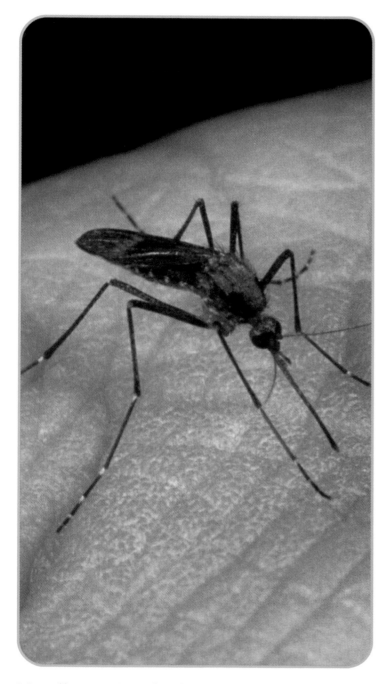

Not all mosquitoes bite! Only certain kinds of mosquitoes bite people and other animals.

Mosquitoes and fleas are insects that bite people and other animals. Insect bites often become red and itchy in the same way that insect stings do. Insect bites also make some people and animals sick.

Did you know?
Only female mosquitoes, shown left, bite people and animals. Female mosquitoes bite to suck up blood. They need blood in order to lay their eggs. Blood has the nutrients that female mosquitoes need for their eggs.

Pesky parasites

Some insects are **parasites**. Parasites live on the skin of animals or inside their bodies. Living things that carry parasites are called **hosts**. Parasites bite their hosts and feed on their bodies or blood. Parasites can make their hosts sick. Parasites do not make the hosts sick on purpose, however. Like all animals, parasites need food and places to live in order to stay alive.

Fleas are parasites that live on the bodies of dogs or cats. Pet owners can give their pets medicines to make sure they will not get fleas.

Spreading diseases

Some biting insects are harmful because they spread **diseases**. Diseases are serious illnesses. Mosquitoes are insects that spread diseases. When a mosquito drinks the blood of an animal with a disease, it can catch the disease from the animal. The mosquito then passes the disease to the next animal or person it bites.

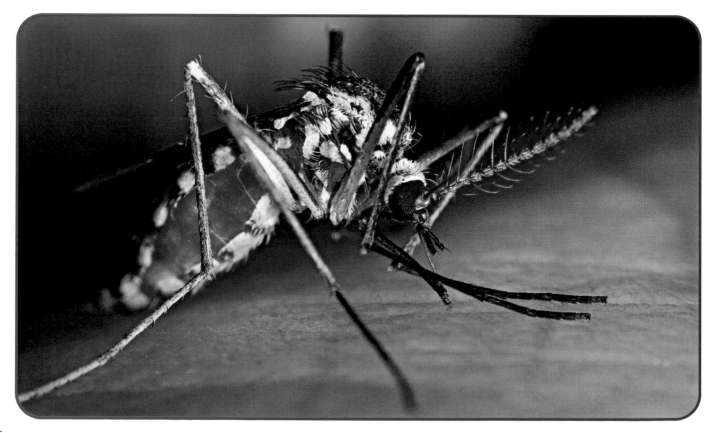

Some fleas carry diseases. A flea that has a disease can spread it to the animals and people it bites.

Did you know?
Mosquitoes can spread dangerous diseases such as typhus, **malaria**, and **West Nile virus** to animals and people. Some of these diseases can be cured or treated. Many people and animals die from these diseases, however.

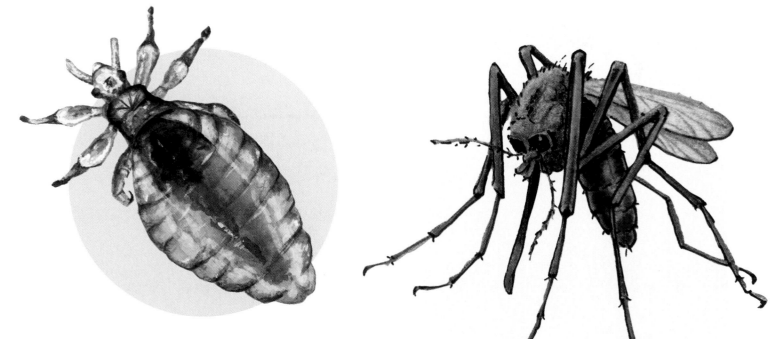

*Some kinds of lice can spread **typhus**. When lice bite people or animals that have typhus, they can spread the disease to the other living things they bite.*

Damage to homes and crops

Some plant-eating insects are harmful to people because they eat wood. These insects can destroy trees and wooden buildings by eating them. Other plant-eating insects are harmful because they feed on crops that people grow for food. These insects often damage the crops.

Wood eaters

Termites, shown left, are insects that eat wood. They damage trees and wooden buildings as they eat. Termites that eat wood live inside the wood that they are eating. They can wreck wooden walls and floors. They sometimes destroy entire houses!

Damaging crops

Some insects feed on potato, corn, fruit, and other crops that farmers grow. The insects damage the crops as they eat. A **swarm** of locusts, shown below, can eat thousands of crops in a matter of hours. A swarm is a large group of moving insects.

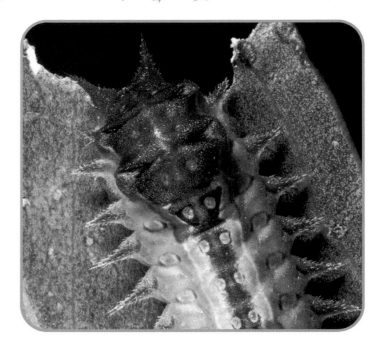

Many types of caterpillars feed on the crops that farmers grow.

Some locust swarms are made up of millions of locusts. The swarms travel long distances, eating many plants along the way.

Create a buzz!

Some insects may seem scary, but they are just trying to stay alive! Certain insects can be harmful to people, but there are many more helpful insects than there are harmful insects!

Post it!

You can teach your family and friends about helpful insects. Make a poster that shows pictures of helpful insects. Then write lists of all the ways these insects are helpful to other living things. The steps on the next page will help you get started.

Get drawing!

Use this book to help you pick one or more helpful insects for your poster. You can draw pictures of insects that pollinate plants, such as butterflies, moths, and bees, and then write about how they help plants. You might want to choose scavengers or draw some of the insects that animals eat. Look at the poster on this page to give you some ideas.

Search the Internet or visit the library to learn about the many other kinds of helpful insects.

The buzz on bees

Honeybees make sweet honey for me to eat.

Honeybees make beeswax that people use to make candles.

Honeybees pollinate flowers and help new plants grow.

Honeybees are food for other animals.

Glossary

Note: Boldfaced words that are defined in the text may not appear in the glossary.

beekeeper A person who raises and cares for honeybees

beeswax A substance that honeybees make inside their bodies

cell A small enclosed space

cocoon A case made of silk that caterpillars spin around themselves before they turn into butterflies or moths

germ A tiny living particle that can make people sick

malaria A disease spread by mosquitoes that causes a high fever

nectar A sweet liquid found in flowers

pollen A powdery substance found in flowers that the flowers need in order to make seeds

silk A strong, thin, sticky fiber that certain caterpillars are able to make inside their bodies

typhus A disease, spread by fleas or other insects, which causes a person to have a fever and a headache

West Nile virus A disease spread by mosquitoes that causes a person to have a fever, a headache, and a rash on his or her skin

Index

1 2 3 4 5 6 7 8 9 0 Printed in the U.S.A. 4 3 2 1 0 9 8 7 6 5